Wheels Around Paisley

by
Robert Grieves

D1439270

Most folks who are of an age to recall the tramcars in Paisley remember them fondly. The municipal Glasgow Corporation Transport Department had operated the Paisley services since 1923 when Paisley District Tramways was acquired. As a boy I often used the trams and was able to take advantage of the incredibly cheap halfpenny special fare when travelling to and from school. The trams were frequent and relatively warm and comfortable since Elderslie depot had a good allocation of the more modern 'Coronation' type cars, one of which (1283) is tackling the climb up St Mirren Brae en route from Glenfield to Renfrew Ferry on service 28, a busy and lucrative route which met competition between Paisley and Renfrew from the buses of Cunninghams, Patons and Western SMT. This view in 1954 looking towards the Cross with Dunn Square on the right also shows a former P&D Guy Arab (XS 6559) on Western's local service to Lochfield, which was always shown on the destination as 'Loch Road' whereas trams which turned there showed 'Lochfield Road'. The cars in the foreground are an Austin A40 'Devon' heading uphill past the Co-op and a Rover 75 at Forbes Place.

© Robert Grieves 2000
First published in the United Kingdom, 2000,
by Stenlake Publishing
Telephone / Fax: 01290 551122

ISBN 1 84033 130 5

THE PUBLISHERS REGRET THAT THEY CANNOT SUPPLY
COPIES OF ANY PICTURES FEATURED IN THIS BOOK.

Yes, even pedal car and pram wheels come within the parameters of this book. The Tri-ang pedal car seen here driven by myself at the 'country' end of Arkleston Road (which amazingly has still escaped housing development) was a Christmas present for three-year-old me in 1947 and was my pride and joy for a year or two before I outgrew it and it then passed to my wee brother. I progressed to home-made bogies manufactured from planks and pram wheels (already I had an eye on those on my brother's pram seen here). Bogies were blessed with many different names (cartie or guider for instance) according to where you lived in Scotland but I remember in Paisley that we usually referred to them as gigs (pronounced geegs). The pram had been mine until my brother came on the scene and this view in the garden at Clydesdale Avenue in February 1948 shows the uncompromising utilitarian lines of 1940s perambulators and the equally uncompromising appearance of myself (centre) and pal Joey McKee from two doors up, wartime utility babies both. Obviously balaclavas were 'in' that season.

FOREWORD

After the cities of Glasgow, Edinburgh, Aberdeen and Dundee, the textile town of Paisley for long came next as Scotland's largest centre of population, until overtaken in recent years by East Kilbride. Although only 6 miles west of Glasgow, Paisley has always been a very independent place and its Buddies very independent people. This little book is not primarily about the town itself but rather the transport which served it and I would hope that the scenes selected will evoke memories for many of the older generation in particular. Hopefully they might kindle a desire in younger folks to find out more about Paisley's past because recent history can prove just as fascinating as the ancient kind. Somewhere among the following pages I hope you find your own special memory of Wheels Around Paisley.

On page 9 is a view of Young's original Meikleriggs horse bus which soldiered on until the outbreak of war in 1914. In the mid-1920s the service was restarted with 14-seat motorbuses of the type shown. This was an American-built Reo which was one of several in the fleets of both the Paisley & District Omnibus Company (which was owned originally by the Fyfe Brothers and based at the foot of Moss Street) and Shankland & Gardiner of Murray Street. Many Buddies referred to the P&D as 'poor & destitute' since the fleet was largely composed of somewhat down-at-heel second-hand vehicles. S&G was also known by an equally derogatory but unprintable description. Both firms built up a network of services around the town, including runs to Meikleriggs, St James' Avenue, Springbank Road, Nethercraigs, Arkleston, Lochfield and Craigielea. In 1933 the Fyfes sold to Young's Bus Service, who continued to operate the Paisley local runs under the title P&D, which they retained as a separate company until sale to Western SMT in 1950. S&G sold direct to Western in 1937 and this scene shows 'Gleniffer', one of their Reo 14-seaters of 1925 with its short-trousered conductor at St James' Avenue before departing for Meikleriggs.

Looking down the High Street towards the Cross and Town Hall, which is just visible on the right. This glimpse of life in the 1890s was seen from where the Marks & Spencer store is today but nowadays, of course, we don't see cattle being herded down the High Street. The buildings at the end of Moss Street to the left were demolished to make way for Paisley's War Memorial which was unveiled in July 1924. One of the Paisley Tramway Company single deck horse trams has just left the Cross to head for the West End terminus at Thomas Street. Also noteworthy is the smart militiaman on the right. Paisley's last horse tram ran in November 1903. (Picture courtesy of Paisley Museum.)

The Paisley Tramway Company Ltd. inaugurated a service of horse-drawn trams between Garthland Place in the east end of the town and Broomlands in the west in December 1885 from a depot in Incle Street. Extensions at each end to Greenlaw and Thomas Street soon followed and a further extension to Hawkhead Road became the company's eastern terminus. This scene from the late 1880s shows a double deck 'knifeboard' style car (so-called because of the back-to-back bench seating arrangement on top) in Glasgow Road, Williamsburgh, heading towards Paisley Cross. The entrance to the Barracks was, at that time, to the left of this scene and is no doubt where the sergeant on the right has come from. The well-remembered Kelburne cinema was later built on the site to the left. (Picture courtesy of Paisley Museum.)

The first electric tramcars to operate in Paisley were those of the Glasgow Corporation Tramways, which initially ran from the city to Hawkhead Road in November, 1903. The horse trams then ceased to function, but it was not until June 1904 that Paisley's own tramway company commenced electric operation between the Cross and Hawkhead Road. This scene in Glasgow Road at Garthland Lane looking east towards the spire of Sherwood Church shows car no. 3 in the foreground and no. 1 in the distance during the first few weeks of service. An excited bunch of boys runs after car 3 which of course was very much a novelty at the time. On the wall of the former horse tram depot, lower left, in Incle Street, may be seen the wording 'Established 1835, Robt. Roxburgh & Sons, Coach Builders, Garthland Carriage Works', with a hand pointing to adjacent Garthland Lane. Additionally, the tramway company advertised 'Broughams, brakes, omnibuses and waggonettes for hire. Also carriages for marriage parties.' St Mirin's Cathedral now stands on this site.

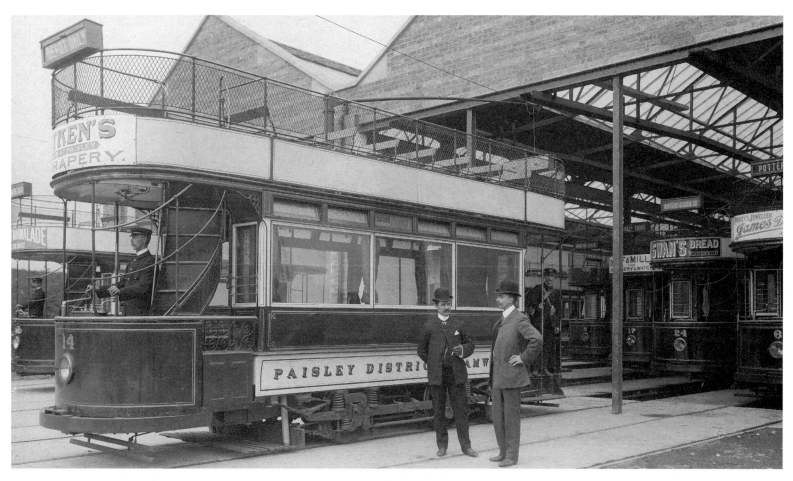

Paisley trams were familiarly known as 'Murphies' by the Buddies, after the company promoter William Murphy who came from the Dublin United Tramway Co. and brought with him several Irish employees to work on the Paisley system. Here we see some of the brand new Murphies at the recently opened depot at Elderslie in 1904, which replaced the old horse tram premises in Incle Street. Although obviously specially posed for the photographer, this is a delightful scene with the drivers at their controls, the conductor on the platform of no. 14 and the tramway company officials wearing the almost obligatory bowler hats of the period. The adverts on the cars feature long-gone local firms: Aitken's Drapery in New Street; Duff & Miller, jewellers and watchmakers, 9 High Street; and Swan's Bread ('sweetest and best'). J. & M. Swan's bakery was at 78 Causeyside. A view of Elderslie depot towards the end of the tramway era may be seen on page 33.

Paisley District Tramways cars carried a resplendent scarlet and ivory livery, as borne here by car no. 1 en route from Renfrew Ferry to Potterhill in 1905 and passing the erstwhile Municipal Buildings in County Square. In addition to the side advert for Van Houten's Cocoa ('best and goes farthest'), another at the front promotes the Paisley Polytechnic which was the High Street drapery owned by Naismith & Scott. A hansom cab awaiting custom at the town rank completes this atmospheric Edwardian scene. Large numbers of these two-wheeled, two-seater cabs (invented by architect Joseph Hansom) operated on the streets of London and other cities. With the arrival of motorised cabs in Edwardian times, the hansoms began to fade from the streets of Paisley.

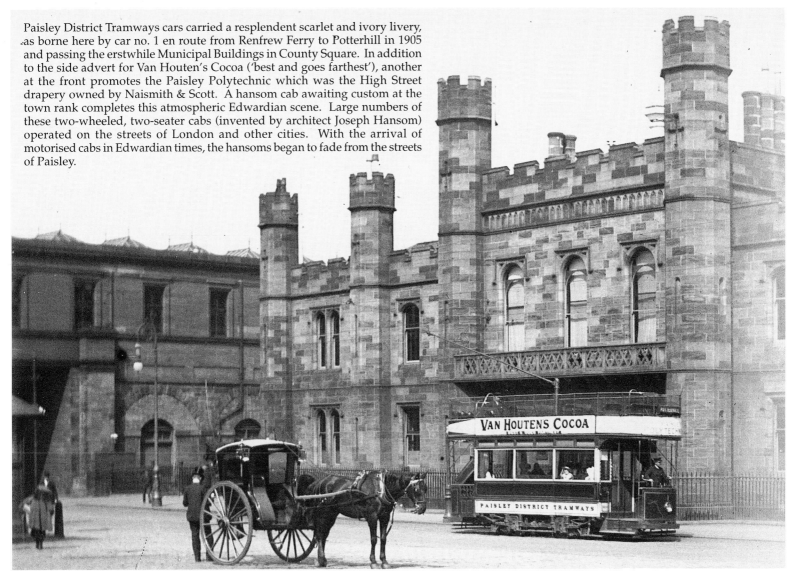

Paisley's main cab rank has been in County Square since Victorian times, and although now in a different area of the square the rank is still adjacent to Gilmour Street station. One of the best-known taxi drivers in Paisley for many years was the late Joe Arlet. Back in the 1920s, the Arlet family was better known for providing the first bus service to Nitshill and also had a presence on the lucrative Glasgow/Paisley/Johnstone bus route along with many other entrepreneurs. Too much competition, however, killed the bus enterprise but the family then entered the taxi trade. This was Joe Arlet's traditional cab in the 1960s – an immaculate white-wall tyred Austin FX3 which had been new in 1950 and had formerly worked in London. It is seen on the rank in County Square with the old post office and Gilmour Street station behind.

A much earlier scene in County Square dating from around 1901 before the tramway company laid its tracks. Looking towards the General Post Office and Gilmour Street railway station buildings we see the evidence proving that the Square has been a cab rank for over a century. The cabbies' rest is prominent and alongside it Young's horse bus (see opposite) awaits departure time for Meikleriggs. It is perhaps not generally appreciated that the original Gilmour Street station, seen clearly in this view, is one of the oldest buildings in the town, dating from the late 1830s. The Glasgow & Paisley Joint Railway opened in 1840.

COUNTY SQUARE, PAISLEY.

William Young, who had originally been a coachman to the Coats family, commenced a horse bus service in the 1890s from County Square via the High Street and on to Meikleriggs, where it is seen in this view at the terminus outside Gleniffer Home. Today the Royal Alexandra Hospital would be visible in the background, but the home itself remains unchanged. The horse bus, with Jimmy its driver, continued in service until March 1914. Later the Young family, who owned riding stables at Stanleymuir Farm on Gleniffer Braes, were to become better known when they commenced motorbus operations between Glasgow, Paisley and Johnstone in the mid-1920s.

Before motor vehicles became more commonplace, virtually all goods were delivered by horse-drawn carts. Naturally most towns provided a sufficient number of horse troughs to satisfy the drouthy beasts. Paisley horses were quite well supplied and this late Victorian scene shows the trough at the top end of Causeyside at its gushet with Neilston Road near Stevenson Street, outside the fleshers shop owned by William Brown junior. A drinking fountain was immediately adjacent where the carter could slake his thirst at the same time. On the other hand, Adam's public house on the left advertises Old Bushmills Irish whiskey, which was possibly a much greater attraction. The entrance to the immediate right of the pub was named Anvil Close. Note also the message boy in traditional delivery pose with basket on head standing to the left of the group watching the well-known local photographer James Brown, who no doubt took a few minutes to set up what was then cumbersome camera apparatus on a tripod in order to photograph this scene.

Horse-drawn funeral processions were quite common even into the 1930s and firms such as Young's in Gordon Street specialised in this business. The carriage seen here in the 1920s was owned by Robert 'Pipie' Patterson of Caledonia Street and later St James' Street who was another established undertaker and carriage hirer in the town. He also had branch offices in Seedhill Road and Wellmeadow, with stables originally in Clark Street and then Lacy Street. Black horses of course were normally provided for funerals and were often additionally decorated with black plumes. Next door to Patterson's office may be seen the Wellington Dairy, whose premises are still in Caledonia Street to this day.

Fred Coutts was the Paisley & District Tramways Company general manager. His artist brother Frank drew these scenes for one of a series of picture postcards issued by the company in 1907. This one includes Parkhead-born engineer John Scott Russell's steam carriage which commenced a short-lived operation between Glasgow and Paisley in April 1834 only to finish abruptly after an accident at Halfway on 29 July the same year. Apparently the boiler did not explode, contrary to common assumption (and Coutts' sketch) but four passengers died from their injuries caused by leaping from the overturning carriage. This could therefore be regarded as Scotland's first fatal automobile accident. Russell is perhaps better known for his later engineering partnership with Isambard Kingdom Brunell in the construction of the steamship *Great Eastern*, launched in 1857.

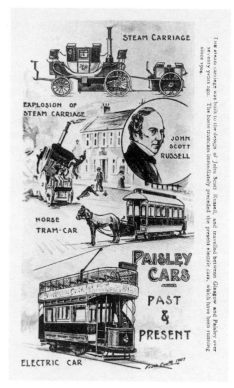

An evocative Edwardian scene showing a bustling Paisley Cross in 1905 with two open-top tramcars visible. To the left is a Glasgow Corporation car about to depart on the lengthy route to the city and then through to Barrachnie in the east end, a journey often taken by Buddies who were curious to discover where this strange sounding destination was located, as it might as well have been Bombay for all they knew. The other is a Paisley car about to turn left into Gilmour Street on its journey from Johnstone to Renfrew Ferry.

Paisley Cross around 1906, at which time photographers still aroused a great deal of interest, owing to the elaborate arrangements they had to carry out in order to capture a successful shot. The assembled crowd here is almost entirely male (and everyone is wearing a hat or cap) but a lady and a group of four schoolgirls enjoy a grandstand view of proceedings from the open top deck of the Paisley District Tramways car at the stop outside James Jack's grocery store (now the site of Burton's menswear shop). This tram has come from Renfrew Ferry and is heading south to Potterhill. The other tram was owned by Glasgow Corporation and would shortly depart on the long service through the city and then via Parkhead to Barrachnie in the eastern suburbs. Glasgow acquired the Paisley & District Tramways Co. in 1923 and continued to operate in the town until 1957. Former Paisley car no. 68 has been restored and preserved in the National Tramway Museum at Crich, Derbyshire. It almost returned home in 1988 when it operated at the Glasgow Garden Festival.

Motor transport in Scotland's largest town was sparse at the start of the twentieth century. Only the wealthy could afford an automobile and even businesses generally depended on horse-drawn transport during the Edwardian era. However in 1902 a manufacturer known as the Mo-Car Syndicate, which produced Arrol-Johnston cars and commercial vehicles, set up business in former mill premises in Underwood after a fire had forced abandonment of their previous works in Glasgow. This company had been largely financed by Sir William Arrol, the engineer who to this day is probably best remembered for the construction of the Forth Railway Bridge in the 1880s. Arrol had been born at Houston in Renfrewshire and had started work at the age of 9 in a thread mill. One of the first companies in Paisley to purchase an Arrol-Johnston was W. P. Robertson's Stonefield Laundry, which placed this primitive-looking 12 h.p. delivery lorry in service in 1903. When motor licensing was introduced in 1904 it was given the Paisley registration number XS 20. A 1912 directory described this laundry as Scotland's largest. Robertson also owned the Bute Steam Laundry in Rothesay.

Robertson's Stonefield Laundry increased their motor fleet in 1929 when XS 2307 was purchased from Karrier Motors of Huddersfield.

Paisley was home to many rival laundry companies in the days before washing machines started to lessen the demand for their services. Among these were Robertson's Stonefield Laundry (featured opposite); James Morton's St George's Laundry in George Place; Alex Morrison's Jenny's Well Laundry; Gibson & Reid's Linside Laundry in Cyril Street; John Lawson's Tannahill Laundry, 21 Castle Street; W. B. Marr's Shortroods Laundry and Wm. Gardner's Holm Laundry in Barterholm. This photo shows XS 2740, a 1931 Ford van in the once-familiar fleet of Bell's Gleniffer Laundry which later moved from their Stanely Dyeworks in Causeyside to modern premises in Hawkhead Road.

Long before the Hillman Imp was built in Linwood in the 1960s and 70s, the Arrol-Johnston car was produced at the previously mentioned Underwood factory in Paisley from 1902 until production moved to Dumfries in 1913. The Paisley premises were in a disused thread mill which had been provided by the Coats family, shareholders in the Mo-Car Syndicate which built the Arrol-Johnston. The car illustrated was the 12/15 h.p. model of 1909. This one had been purchased by a family in Roxburghshire and is seen cooling down after reaching the summit of the Devil's Elbow road between Blairgowrie and Braemar which was a true test of automobile stamina in those pioneering days of motoring.

In the early days of motoring, automobiles were owned almost exclusively by the more affluent members of the community as in real terms cars cost much more then than now. Archibald Fulton Craig, the Paisley engineer, is seen here on what would appear to be a picnic outing (note the basket on the roof) in his chauffeur-driven Rolls Royce limousine with the Paisley number XS 6, which judging by the crumpled front offside mudguard had been involved in an accident. A. F. Craig & Co. Ltd. produced a variety of machinery at their factory in MacDowall Street including petroleum distillation and refining equipment, carpet looms, boilers, iron castings and sugar refining machinery. (Picture courtesy of David Rowand.)

In addition to Arrol-Johnston, Paisley boasted another couple of motor manufacturers in Edwardian days, although on a much smaller scale. These were James McGeoch's Abercorn Carriage and Motor Company of Mill Street who built light three-wheel two-seaters named Seetstu, which of course was a play on words from Seestu, the old name for Paisley. The other Paisley-built car was the Ridley, also a light two-seater produced by John Ridley of George Place from about 1906 to 1910. Illustrated here is a Ridley car which was owned in 1910 by Donald MacLean of Peatriggend House, Slamannan, Stirlingshire.

The Arrol-Johnston Company moved car production from Underwood to a new factory in Dumfries in 1913. However the factory continued to be used for motor vehicle construction under the ownership of Beardmore Motors, who used the Paisley premises to build taxi-cabs, light lorries and small 14-seater buses. A typical Beardmore bus was this locally-owned example which belonged to Robert Sutherland of Barrhead and operated between Barrhead and Paisley in opposition to the Glasgow Corporation tramcars which also plied the same route. This bus, like so many others in the 1920s, had its own distinctive name, in this case 'Excelsior'. It was new in 1925 and licensed HS 4001 in Renfrewshire.

The biggest and best-known bus operator in the Paisley area was Young's Bus Service of Gordon Street. The Young family had started with horse-drawn vehicles (see page 9) in Queen Victoria's reign and also specialised in both funeral undertaking and taxi hire. When the operation of motorbuses became a lucrative proposition in the mid-1920s, Young's joined the fray on the busy Glasgow/Paisley/Johnstone route, quickly building a reputation for good service which many of their rivals lacked. A fleet of mainly Albion buses was built up over the years. These were built at Scotstoun and like Young's Bus Service had an excellent reputation for reliability (their motto was 'Sure as the Sunrise'). Here we see XS 3148, one of the YBS Albion 'Valiant' saloons of 1933 which was then the last word in comfort. It has just left the stop at the Cross and is heading for Glasgow past Urquhart's confectionery shop at the corner of Lawn Street and Gauze Street. In the background is Robert Cochran's outfitters store which is now Arnott's.

Gauze Street looking towards Glasgow Road from the Cotton Street junction in the mid-1950s. Most of the wheels in this scene belong to public transport. The Western SMT bus in the foreground is heading for Arkleston Road on the Paisley circular service which operated for many years serving Ferguslie Park, Craigielea, Gallowhill, Arkleston and Lochfield in both directions. The Glasgow Corporation 'Cunarder' type tramcar makes its way towards the terminus at Elderslie, while the Albion bus owned by Western is on the lengthy journey from Glasgow to Ayr via Troon, a service which operated every half hour, but like so many others has since been completely abandoned. The three shops visible in Cotton Street are Charles Wilson butchers; Anne Stalker ladies' wear and Galbraiths grocery store. (Photo by Ian Coonie.)

Where bus services were concerned, the most colourful period in the town was undoubtedly the second half of the 1920s, when literally dozens of small operators served Paisley and most particularly the busy service between Glasgow and Johnstone in competition with the Corporation tramcars, where potentially high earnings were to be made. During this period, prior to licensing brought about by the 1930 Road Traffic Act, it was a virtual free-for-all as regards the bus services. The buses themselves were all shapes, sizes and colours and usually bore their own names (see page 19). Seen here at the stance for Paisley and Johnstone buses in Clyde Street, Glasgow, is an imported Reo from the USA which was owned by Alphonso (Jake) Fella, an Italian chip shop owner from Sandholes in the West End. It was unusual for a service bus since it boasted a canvas hood which could be folded back on fine days. Known locally as the 'covered wagon', it was new in 1926 and registered XS 1711. Close inspection shows the Reo badge, with 'St Mirren' and 'Paisley' painted on the bodywork, which had been built by old-established Glasgow coachbuilder Robert Mitchell of Shaftesbury Street, Cranstonhill. The circular disc on the windscreen bears the initials S. W. which alerted passengers to the fact that the bus was part of the South Western Bus Operators' Association, which meant that return tickets were interchangeable on any bus bearing this sign. The drivers on this occasion were Jimmy Fraser (left) and William McLellan, both of whom like many others worked for several of the bus owners of the period. A former conductor on the 'covered wagon' is octogenarian Bert Reid who still lives in the town and who spent much of his working life on the buses, later with Graham of Hawkhead and Western SMT.

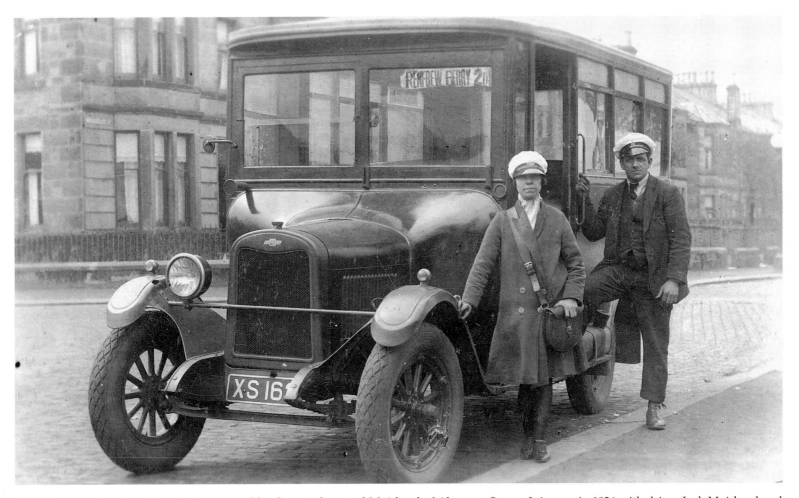

XS 1636 was a 14-seater Chevrolet bus owned by Cunningham and Muirhead of Abercorn Street. It is seen in 1926 with driver Jock Muirhead and conductress Peggy Cunningham at the Paisley terminus of the service to Renfrew Ferry, which at that time was St James' Avenue, adjacent to the racecourse. Cunningham's buses continued to ply between Paisley and Renfrew until selling out to the giant Western SMT Co. in 1979. Their former garage in Underwood Road is now occupied by David Dean's 'Classique' coaches, specialising in tours to the Scottish Highlands and Islands. Cunningham operated coaches with the fleetname 'Ivanhoe' and – usually when he had enjoyed a refreshment or two – Jimmy Cunningham would command anyone who cared to listen, 'Wherever you go, take an Ivanhoe!'. Note the fare from Paisley to Renfrew Ferry which at that time was tuppence.

Young's Bus Service effectively fought off all opposition to become the sole operator on the Glasgow/Johnstone corridor apart from Western SMT, which ran to the coast, and Glasgow Corporation, which served Kilbarchan from Abbotsinch with double-deckers which were garaged at their Elderslie tram depot. One of the post-war Leyland Titans in the YBS fleet was XS 6910, (no. 183), caught by the camera heading down the High Street en route for Glasgow and passing La Scala cinema, which that day in 1950 was showing *Mighty Joe Young* (no relation to YBS) starring Ben Johnson. Young's buses carried a colourful rich yellowy orange livery with maroon and cream relief. This bus was delivered in 1950, just a few months before the company was sold to Western SMT in whose fleet it remained for many years (see page 35).

When Young's Bus Service sold out in 1950 another local bus company took advantage of the situation by purchasing a large quantity of the YBS orange paint which had become surplus. Graham's Bus Service, based in Hawkhead Road and formerly at Linwood Toll until the mid-1930s, had originally used a red livery but decided to change to avoid confusion with the red Western buses which were now operating the local routes. Graham's main service linked Hawkhead, Paisley and Linwood and continued to do so until the company relinquished the business in 1990. Especially during the 1950s and 60s Graham's operated a fleet of mainly Guy Arab double-deckers, one of which (second-hand from Birmingham Corporation) deals with the queue for Linwood at the Cross in the late fifties. (Photo by Ian MacLean.)

Another second-hand Guy Arab in Graham's fleet. This was one of several purchased from Southampton Corporation to cope with fleet expansion after their service frequency increased when the Rootes Group came to Linwood to build the Hillman Imp in 1963. This scene in Queen Street shows no. 55 on a school run delivering the children to the former St Mary's School. Robert Tannahill's thatched cottage is just visible behind the bus.

Smith's Bus Service of Aurs Road, Barrhead, operated from Nitshill and Todholm via Blackhall to their Paisley terminus in Cotton Street. In this scene from the early 1960s, two of their dark green and cream liveried Leylands are seen leaving the town via Orchard Street and Lonend. Today this Bridge Street junction has been considerably altered and the greatly increased traffic flow is controlled by lights. From independent beginnings in the 1920s, James Smith sold his business to the Scottish Co-operative Wholesale Society in 1947, which retained the Smith name until in turn selling out to the acquisitive Western SMT in 1968.

Until the mid-1960s, the middle of St James' Street from Glen Lane to Caledonia Street was used as a bus terminus by several operators for their services to Renfrew, Govan and Barrhead. The first two of these four Leylands, photographed in 1963, were owned by Paton Brothers of Renfrew, the next one by McGill of Barrhead and the last by Western SMT. Today the street is still recognisable from this scene, but now has a raised central reservation area. This view looks west towards the spire of St James' Church in Underwood Road.

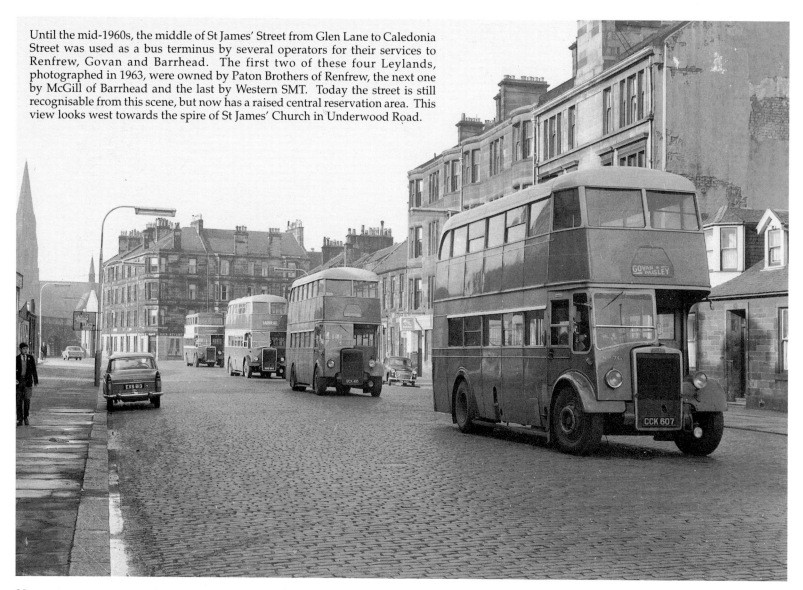

Buddies experienced their first whiff of steam from a railway engine as long ago as 1837 when the unusual 4' 6" gauge line opened between Hamilton Street in Paisley and Renfrew Wharf. Paradoxically, the locomotives were sold and replaced by horses only five years later. This view from British Railways days in July 1958 shows locomotive no. 40636 with the 5.36 p.m. train from Renfrew, which was used mainly by employees of the Babcock & Wilcox engineering works who boarded at Renfrew (South) Station at the foot of Porterfield Road. It is seen calling at Paisley (Abercorn) and is about to pass below the bridge on Renfrew Road, from where the photo was taken. To the right are the buildings of the newly built Reid Kerr College. The outline of the former trackbed is still clearly visible today from the bridge, but the railway station buildings have long gone and Great Mills is now to the left. Abercorn station dated from 1866 when the Paisley & Renfrew Railway was altered to 4' 8½" standard gauge. This line closed in 1967. (Picture courtesy of W.A.C. Smith.)

Paisley's main railway station in Gilmour Street originally opened for business in 1840. When photographed in October 1964, steam operation still ruled but its days were numbered as diesels started to arrive in the mid-1960s. Here we see 2-6-4 tank engine no. 42264 pulling into platform 1 with the 2.05 p.m. from Gourock to Glasgow Central. Although this scene is still recognisable now, the signal box and semaphore signals have long since gone and today's lines to Gourock and to Ayr have been electrified. (Photo courtesy of W.A.C. Smith.)

The old Paisley and Johnstone Canal closed in 1882 and was drained to provide the trackbed for the G&SWR railway line from Glasgow (St Enoch). This scene from August 1963 shows 2-6-4 tank no. 80021 calling at Canal Street station with the 6.48 p.m. from Kilmacolm to St Enoch. In January 1983 the Canal line closed to passenger traffic, only to be reopened in July 1990 after much pleading from the public. The sections heading west from Paisley to Kilmacolm and beyond remained closed, however. (Picture courtesy of W.A.C. Smith.)

A recent photo taken in 2000 but one which includes a great deal of railway history. Seen between Canal Street and Hawkhead station near Blackhall from the Jenny's Well walkway, it shows what is believed to be the oldest bridge anywhere in the world which still actively carries a railway. This bridge was originally constructed in 1810 as an aqueduct to carry the Glasgow, Paisley & Johnstone Canal over the River Cart and after the draining of the canal was converted to carry the new railway line in 1885. The class 101 diesel multiple unit train is also of interest as the 'slam door' rolling stock was amongst the oldest surviving in daily use anywhere in Britain, having been built in the late 1950s. Visible in the background is the empty shell of Clark's Anchor threadmill at Seedhill.

Coronation type tramcars (which were introduced during 1937 when King George VI came to the throne) are represented in this 1957 view of the no. 28 terminus, known as Glenfield. This was the final year of tramway operation in Paisley. Glenfield Road runs off to the right and partly visible is Alex Morton's wooden kiosk which sold sweets and lemonade to folk going for a walk 'up the Braes' and also of course to thirsty tram crews. In this view, looking in the direction of Barrhead, car 1281 has just arrived while 1277 (foreground) departs down to Potterhill en route for Renfrew Ferry. This was to be the very last car in service on the final day of trams in Paisley – Saturday 11 May 1957 – although it was early on the Sunday morning before 1277 reached Elderslie depot, having contended with a large and sentimental crowd all the way from Renfrew Ferry.

Elderslie tram depot also garaged the Glasgow Corporation buses on service 12 which operated between Kilbarchan and Abbotsinch. Some of these may be seen in this view of the depot, which also shows Standard type car no. 941 and the remains of a burned out Standard amongst whose shell some small boys are playing. Elderslie depot was the 'graveyard' for retired Corporation trams, as they were brought there to be scrapped. This view looks towards Newton Terrace on the main Paisley/Johnstone road and the railway arches at Howe Street.

Gauze Street at its junction with Cotton Street in the late 1940s. Both during and after World War II, the Paisley & District Omnibus Co. purchased Guy Arab double-deckers to replace elderly second-hand Leyland vehicles which had reached the end of their days. P&D no. 288 (XS 5722) was acquired in 1946 and is seen on the Ferguslie Park/Gallowhill/Arkleston/Lochfield/Ferguslie Park service, known to the bus crews as 'the circle'.

A late 1950s view of Bridge Street from the roundabout where it met Orchard Street and Johnston Street, a far cry from today's busy junction controlled by traffic lights. Apart from the famous twelfth century Abbey dominating the skyline, a familiar sight for many years was Hamilton's garage, which later became 'The Garage' and then 'Pravda' discotheque. All buses which served the coast were re-routed via Cotton Street and Canal Street during the 1950s away from the Cross and the congested High Street. Leyland XS 6910 had originally been delivered to Young's Bus Service of nearby Gordon Street in 1950 (see page 24) but was acquired with the rest of the fleet by Western SMT shortly afterwards.

Young's bus depot and also that of their subsidiary Paisley & District Omnibus Co. was at 4 Gordon Street, originally the site of the stables for Young's cab and funeral horses. Founder of the business, William Young, had originally been coachman to the Coats family of thread fame and after starting business on his own account kept horses at livery in the Gordon Street stables. A contemporary Edwardian advertisement offered 'Saddle hacks and hunters, also chargers for officers and yeomanry and ponies for boys and girls. Broughams, victorias, landaus and polo carts for hire, also modern rubber tyred hearses and funeral carriages.' After Young's sold out to Western SMT in the early 1950s, Western continued to use the Gordon Street premises as a bus depot as did their successor, Clydeside Scottish Omnibuses, until 1992 by which time it had become extremely difficult to manoeuvre from the narrow pend into the busy flow of traffic. This scene from around 1960 shows two Western buses leaving the depot adjacent to the Causeyside Street junction, where there were no traffic lights at that time. The buildings to the right were demolished for the street to be widened, but the old depot remains as yet an abandoned site awaiting purchase.

Looking down High Street from New Street corner in 1951. The public transport in this scene was all owned by the Glasgow Corporation Transport Department who operated both trams and buses from their depot at Elderslie until 1957. The trams are seen on service 21 which ran from Elderslie via Paisley to Anniesland, while the no. 12 bus served the route between Abbotsinch and Kilbarchan. Seen here is an AEC Regent (A113 – FYS 213) which had been new in 1949, while the split windscreen Morris Minor convertible was a 1950 model. Other vehicles in view include a 1949 Jowett Bradford station wagon parked outside Cooper's grocery store and a 1946 Morris Commercial lorry delivering to Stanley Bros. (drapers). High Street shops visible include Smart & Rolland (tailors and outfitters); Cable Shoes; A. L. Scott (shoes); Andrew Gibson (baker and tea-room); Woolworths; MacDuff (chemist and optician); R. S. McColl (confectioner); and Campbell Horsburgh (chemist and photographic supplies) who also sold Dinky toys and where as a schoolboy my first model cars and buses were purchased. The Commercial Bank of Scotland occupied the corner site at Moss Street.

A most unusual wheeled vehicle in Paisley was this 1919 Albion A10 model which after many years work on the streets as a conventional lorry with a Co-operative Society was fitted with flanged wheels and converted to run on railway tracks. It was used to shunt wagons containing bitumen for road surfacing on a private track connecting Richard Smith's Craigielea chemical works and tar distillery in Clark Street to the main Glasgow/Gourock railway line. It still carried its original registration number GA 1453 and continued in use until well into the 1950s.

Also of strange appearance was this 1920s left-hand drive model T Ford which had been specially lengthened and fitted with unusually small wheels to permit loading and unloading at the bays within Clark's Anchor Mills. The bodywork was built by David Smith, who had originated in Victorian times as a cartwright and blacksmith in Galloway Street off Underwood Road. The firm is still in business there today specialising in welding and metal fabrication. In the background of this view against the railway dividing wall are some examples of horse-drawn carts built by Smith.

Galbraith's Stores was a household name in the Paisley area for over half a century. John Galbraith started with a single shop in Napier Street, Linwood village and grew to become one of the main provision merchants in the west of Scotland, later becoming a member of the Allied Suppliers group which subsequently changed its name to 'Safeway'. From their Paisley premises Galbraith's operated a fleet of over 100 platform lorries and bakery vans supplying their shops with groceries, meat and vegetables from their own warehouses. XS 7447 was typical of many lorries in the fleet. It was an Albion Chieftain which had been new in 1951 and is seen in the loading bay of the non-perishable stores in Back Sneddon Street.

One of Galbraith's original motorised delivery vehicles, a ubiquitous model T Ford of the early 1920s which was bodied in the town by coachbuilder Robert Lawrie of New Sneddon Street.

Among the well-known brand names based in Paisley were Robertson's 'Golden Shred' marmalade in Stevenson Street, Smith's potato crisps in East Lane and Brown & Polson in Falside Road. This view shows the Brown & Polson transport fleet in 1938 outside their factory which today is occupied by Bestfoods (UK) Ltd. Nearest the camera is a three-wheeler James Handyvan, built by the James Cycle Co. of Birmingham. A Bedford is next and then four Albion tipper lorries, all of which were used on grain deliveries from Glasgow docks to the Falside cornflour works.

Fruit merchant Thomas Colquhoun upgraded his delivery fleet in 1954 when he bought XS 8974, an underfloor engined Albion Claymore lorry. Contemporary Albion advertising described it as a 'revolutionary new cab design giving a low unobstructed floor and easy access'. This scene was taken opposite Colquhoun's premises in Cotton Street looking towards the Abbey and Town Hall.

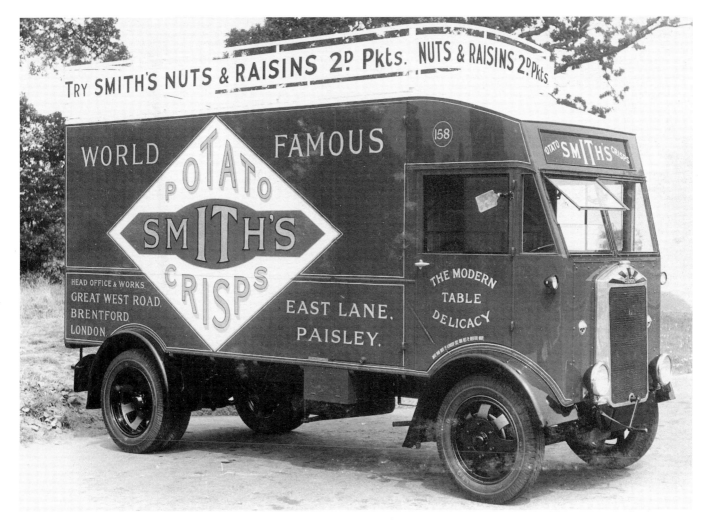

Smith's Crisps were first sold in 1920 and are still a popular brand. Although based in London, Frank Smith soon became a regular customer for Albion delivery vehicles, built at Scotstoun. He opened several branch factories as business progressed and Smith's depot in Paisley was in business from the mid-1920s until the 1970s. It is now occupied by McCormick Foods (Europe) Ltd. This Albion van was new in 1937 and based at the East Lane premises for deliveries in the west of Scotland area.

The Young family branched into road haulage in 1933 when they commenced Young's Express Deliveries, with their lorry fleet based in Portman Street, Glasgow near Paisley Road Toll. This picture shows a YED Albion 6-wheel lorry taking part in a charity parade of floats in the late 1930s. The participating vehicles were lined up in Caledonia Street prior to departure outside the Fountain Gardens. Just visible in the foreground is one of Porrelli's ice cream vans, whose premises were then at 1 Lawn Street. Note the once-familiar Albion 'rising sun' trademark painted on the lorry radiator. The YED fleet was finished in a green and red livery as opposed to Young's orange bus fleet. Other depots were set up in Manchester, Birmingham, Edinburgh, London, Inverness and Kirkcaldy for long-distance trunk operations. Young's Express Deliveries was eventually nationalised and acquired by British Road Services in 1949.

Surely one of Scotland's most unusual shipbuilders must have been Millen Bros. of Paisley. It was impossible for any of the vessels built at their Saucel works in Lonend to be launched from the yard, which was situated well away from the nearest navigable stretch of the River Cart. The majority were constructed in sections and carried to the docks by heavy haulage (as shown), and then exported. Millen's were also constructional engineers, tank-makers and general sheet metal workers. Passing Sherwood Church in Glasgow Road in 1946 is a hopper barge destined for Iceland via Glasgow docks. It was conveyed in two sections by John (Bubbly) Young & Co. of Kelvinhaugh, Glasgow on one of his former American forces Diamond 'T' tank transporters. In the distance the other half of the barge is borne by a Foden. Note the man sitting on top to make sure the load squeezes safely beneath the tramway wires.

Below: Carefully negotiating the turn from Albion Street to Love Street, adjacent to the St Mirren football ground, is a Leyland Badger prime mover owned by haulage contractor J. & M. Taylor of Murray Street and hauling a 45 foot 'trombone' trailer. The huge load was a heat exchanger being transported from the MacDowall Street foundry (known as the Caledonia Engine Works) of engineers A. F. Craig & Co. Ltd. to an oil refinery at Bolsover near Chesterfield. Taylors' were involved with many such large jobs for Craig's who employed over 600 at peak production of diverse machinery and castings. The town sadly lost this major employer in the 1980s. Another vanished Paisley business is Stirrat's dairy, seen behind the lorry. The Taylor family had started a contracting business at Moss-side, Greenock Road about 1850 and progressed to become one of the best known haulage contractors in Paisley. Today the company has diversified to other fields and is now known as J. & M. Taylor (Holdings) Ltd. They have preserved one of their 1947 Albion lorries as a nostalgic reminder of a past era. This photograph was taken in 1971 which means that the toddler on the trike will now be around 30 years of age.

Above: For many years, one of the most familiar vehicles to be seen around the town was GB 27, a little red model T Ford lorry whose registration bore the initials of its owner, Gavin Baird of Henderson Street. Used by him for general carrying work and light removals, both Gavin and his lorry were local institutions well into the 1960s when at last they both retired. It is not clear what became of the 1920s 'tin lizzie', as model Ts were known, but it is believed to have been saved for preservation – a tribute both to Henry Ford and Gavin Baird. It is seen in the late 1950s making a delivery in Clydesdale Avenue.

XS 4797, a three-wheel rotating brush street sweeper built by Lacre in Welwyn Garden City, Herts and purchased by Paisley Burgh Cleansing Department in 1938. This vehicle specialised in keeping the roadside gutters clean.

Delivered during wartime to the Cleansing Department in 1944, XS 5578 was an articulated bin lorry powered by the popular three-wheel Scammell three ton mechanical horse. Over 20,000 of these chassis were built in Watford, Herts from 1933 until replaced by the post-war 'Scarab'.

Paisley Corporation Cleansing Department started to replace their fleet of horse-drawn refuse wagons with motor vehicles in the 1940s, but some continued in use until the 1950s. Seen here at the Underwood Road depot is wagon no. 1 shortly before its withdrawal from service. It was hauled by a well-groomed Clydesdale horse, as were the other wagons. The driver's name is unknown. Some of these men were subsequently trained as motor drivers but others had no wish to do so and were found alternative employment within the department.

What could only have been a Saturday afternoon at Paisley Cross after a St Mirren home match in the days when the Love Street club commanded somewhat greater support than today. This scene from the mid-1950s shows the crowd returning home after the match, some of them aboard a Western SMT Daimler double-decker heading up the High Street en route for Lounsdale Drive when this was possible before today's pedestrianisation. The number on the 1953 Morris about to turn left down St Mirren Brae is XS 8097.